Hello God, Am I Getting Through?

exploring the puzzle and power of prayer

WILL TURNER

Hello God, Am I Getting Through?
exploring the puzzle and power of prayer

Copyright © 1991
Will Turner

All rights reserved. No part of this book may be reproduced in any form–except for the inclusion of brief quotations in a review–without permission in writing from the author or his authorized representative.

First Edition

Printed in the USA
by Morris Publishing
Kearney, NE

1994

Dedication

To my cherished grandchildren:
Jeff
Beth
Shauna
Heather
Brandon
Brett
Christopher
Kelsey
Katie
And to Betty with love.

Contents

Preface...i
Chapter I..1
Strolling Through Uncertainty
Chapter II..7
Where Are You God?
Chapter III...11
Show Us a Miracle, Lord
Chapter IV...17
And God Said, "That's Good"
Chapter V..25
The Substance of Things Hoped for
Chapter VI...31
The Man Called Jesus
Chapter VII...42
Learning to Live with Prayer
Chapter VIII..53
Receipts for Communication
Chapter IX..58
Ambulances and Guardrails
Chapter X...64
The Here and Now
Chapter XI..68
Person-to-Person Call for God

PREFACE

What am I doing here?
If my memory is reliable, that short clause is extracted from a popular song of long ago.

Regardless of the source or the era, it is a question I've asked many times as I prepared and wrote this book about prayer. One's relationship with God is such a personal thing; the subject of religion is so sensitive. My awareness of these facts created a breeding ground for the seeds of uncertainty, and a nagging feeling that I was wading through water far over my head. I often reasoned that the old adage, *Let well enough alone,* is a good slogan to live by. And I consoled myself with a glib analogy:

> I am not a skilled carpenter, so I must rely on someone else to build my house. In much the same way, it would be simple to let someone else do my praying. Without learning the skill myself, or being unable to learn it, I could forever rely on a trained prayer person — a pastor, for example — to intercede on my behalf with the Almighty.

Feeding my mind on the carpenter comparison, however, was merely an escape from guilt. Unlike carpentry, the technique of positive prayer can be quickly mastered by nearly everyone. It is not a skill reserved for the learned scholar or the trained theologian. With a little understanding, a bit of practice, and an infinite amount of patience and faith, prayer is a tool for everyone.

Not only did rejecting the carpenter analogy spur me on, it also marked the beginning of a strange phenomenon. As soon as I extended my antenna into the field of prayer, material seemed to forever fall at my feet. It appeared in most unlikely, perhaps coincidental, places: A book conveniently lying on a hostess's coffee table after a bridge game. An impromptu lunch with a friend who just happened to open a dialogue on the subject of divine intervention. Myriad news and magazine items that regularly popped up when I was writing.

I do not imply that these occurrences were miracles. But I experienced a tingling awareness of a great power that is active in our world — a power whose full potential is too often neglected. This power, under full pressure, is on standby for everyone who wants to make his or her life easier, richer, and more productive.

My book is purposely short. It is not a scholarly treatise. It is not a textbook. It is a layperson's guide to a prayer-driven, God-directed life.

Authors usually thank people who have helped to produce a book. Without using names I thank them now:

Scores of friends contributed, many without knowing it, and some of them from fifty years ago when I was a child far removed from ever writing a book.

Associates and mentors from my contemporary environment, unaware they were contributing, will realize it when they read the book. (Please think of me as grateful, but not sneaky.)

Many rich ideas were gleaned from our learned pastor and scribbled in the margin of the church bulletin so I would remember when I returned to my keyboard.

With genuine appreciation, I thank members of my creative writing classes who thought I was teaching *them*. Perhaps I was in a small way, but in the process it was they who motivated me to press forward — to practice the things I preached to them.

In final evaluation, it is readers who make a book succeed or flop. To all of you, Dear Readers, whoever you are, wherever you may be, I say:

Read, enjoy, pray, and profit.

CHAPTER ONE

A STROLL THROUGH UNCERTAINTY

Give Me a Place to Stand and I Can Move the World
— Archimedes

This book is about prayers and praying.

I think I hear you saying, "Hey, I grew up on prayers. Who needs another book?"

In a way, you are right. Most of us bow our heads in church at least once a week. In times of calamity or grief, we may even kneel to give our prayers an added boost. Having had these experiences, you will be shocked — or even angry — when I suggest that your praying may be a half-conscious habit based on faulty methods and fuzzy conceptions. Or, even worse, it could be doomed to failure before it ever gets out of the transmitter.

Let's take a little test:

Do you digest every word of your minister's prayers from the pulpit?

Do you repeat the Lord's prayer with fervor, concentrating on its rich, encouraging sentences?

If you answered *yes* to both questions, I owe you an apology. If you answered *no* you are eligible for membership in *SAM, Society of the Apathetic Majority.*

Welcome to the organization, but let's get out of it as soon as possible.

DOES PRAYER REALLY WORK?

As a preacher's kid, I had hundreds of opportunities to observe prayer in action.

Demands made on God covered the spectrum of human wants and worldly needs.

"Make us better people, O Lord."
"Send rain for our thirsty crops."
"Heal our sick neighbor."
"Watch over us on our long journey, Lord, and protect those who are left behind."

Did these supplications work? Possibly. Even in 1932, when sea voyages were hazardous, Father Murphy, the local Catholic priest, traveled with our prayers from South Dakota to Ireland and safely home again. Most people, even we non-Catholics, believed our prayers went with him.

Marriages in those days were always sealed with a prayer. Most unions remained intact, but divorce was uncommon when I was growing up in rural America.

Soon after a prayer for moisture, rain often fell on thirsty crops. Farmers were confident their pleas had been answered.

At prayer meeting on Wednesday nights, parishioners gave God a full report on *evil-goings-on* in the community. Some of those immoral conditions corrected themselves. Others hung around for fifty years to haunt later generations. Prayers for sick neighbors were commonplace. Some pulled through. Some died. I often wondered how God decided whom to save and whom to let go. With the simplicity of a child, however, I accepted God's wonders and assumed he had a fair way to work out these sticky problems. In retrospect, I may have been impatient with him for not sending me a tricycle, but I never doubted that *he could have done it if he'd really set his mind to it.*

At this point, I offer a disclaimer: I am neither a theologian nor a scholar. As I write about prayer, I am drawing on personal observations, a few case histories, and considerable research. Particularly, I am revealing experiences which I shall describe as honestly and accurately as possible.

Having traveled the exploratory route, my greatest concern in describing the journey is the need for surety, consistency, and logic — difficult elements to fuse and keep in balance. I walked in a tangled forest of mystery — a place inhabited by improbable *facts.* Because I have been trained to seek cause and effect relationships I expected that spiritual manifestations should repeat themselves in similar sets of circumstances. They haven't and they don't; yet, spiritual manifestations do occur.

How then can one make positive declarations about divine interventions?

Sometimes I felt like the pastor who wrote in the margin of his sermon, "Weak point. Yell real loud."

Whenever I was prepared to phrase a firm conclusion, a tiny inner voice — and sometimes a chorus of external voices — demanded, *PROVE IT.*

Most theologians and many lay people quote chapter and verse from the Bible as ultimate proof. I'm sorry, I cannot do that. For me to say, "This I know for the Bible tells me so," would be a *copout,* a textbook example of *question-begging. Argument in a circle.*

The Bible is a distinguished literary masterpiece, probably the world's greatest historical novel. Its documented accuracy is impressive, but, as a source of factual proof, the *Good Book* cannot be admitted, verbatim, to the court of religious inquiry.

In spite of this assertion, to clarify and reinforce my statements, I may now and then refer to Biblical passages, particularly as they relate to the verifiable role of Jesus Christ. But, in our exploration of prayer, there can be no ultimate proof. Only the testimony of experiment and experience will prevail.

Personal prayer — **power prayer** — is what we are searching for, and we shall discover its explosive potential in the mind and soul of us all.

Here are some specific goals I have tried to reach:

to prove we can actually communicate with God on a consistent basis.

to discover the best methods for making connection with him.

to demonstrate that significant results, do indeed, occur.

Notice that I often refer to God as **HIM**. This is purely for the sake of grammatical convenience. I do not believe that God has either shape or gender. At times I may even say **IT**, or **THE SPIRIT**, or perhaps **THE UNIVERSAL MIND**.

Whatever designation I use, you may always be certain that I mean **GOD**.

AN ELUSIVE QUEST

Prayer in my life has often been a fuzzy cloud floating halfway between my unreachable subconscious and my unattended conscious mind. I admit to harboring heretical thoughts:

> **Prayer is a voodoo superstition.**
> **Prayer is like a little boy leading his invisible dog.**
> **You might as well talk to your shadow.**

Fortified with these *truths*, Sunday morning prayers in church soon became little more than droning accompaniment for next week's planning session. By putting my brain in neutral, I was absolved from exerting any intellectual activity. Then, slowly it occurred to me that I was relying on *prayer by proxy*. I had relegated my conscience to the village pastor and wasn't even auditing his stewardship.

MORE HERESY

During a middle period of my life, when I pondered the matter — as I honestly did now and then — I concluded that prayer was a useless ritual, and any appearance of answered prayer was a mere coincidence. Therefore, if I wasn't receiving the tangible rewards I asked for, why fool around asking for them in the first place?

I honestly admit that when I did pray, some of my requests were pretty silly. I once asked God to help me extract a raise from my boss. He refused. A few days later my wounds of disappointment became badly infected when I learned that one of my colleagues had received a substantial boost in pay and had even jumped two steps up the salary scale. This guy had never prayed for anything in his whole life.

And I am sure Mark Twain had him in mind when he wrote, "Some of his words were not Sunday School words."

This event, coupled with a few others, forced me to conclude that God was either unfair to loyal clients, or careless in processing his messages.

THE SEARCH REVIVED

Having revealed these things how can I possible write a book on prayer? If that question is bothering you, let me explain: Secretly — at times unconsciously — I am intrigued by mysterious things. Because prayer is a mystery, I was impelled to explore it.

I had to discover whether prayer has power and potential.

I had to test ways for communicating with God on a reliable basis.

I had to learn whether he really listens.

Notice I've said nothing about proving there is a God. I am compelled to accept his living presence. Archimedes once said, "Give me a place to stand, and I can move the World." God is my platform. If there were no God — or if he is dead — prayer would be useless, and this book could end here and now. God's existence is a moot question.

My only concerns are:

Where does he hang out? How can I reach him?

Judging from the things he has built and the jobs he has accomplished, God must have fantastic creative power.

Can we share that power?

Can we tap it to improve our lives and enhance our performance?

Can we chat with God in a very personal way?

Does he listen and respond?

In essence, I needed to find out if I could *ring him up* as we used to say in the old days of hand-cranked telephones.

After exploring the subject of prayer experimentally and objectively, I uncovered some principles of faith — some techniques — for contacting *the man/the woman/the spirit* upstairs.

My voyage has helped me to answer the question, "**Hello God, Am I getting through?**"

And in writing about it, and reading about it, I hope we can discover, together, what prayer can do for all of us.

CHAPTER TWO

WHERE ARE YOU, GOD?

Is the abode of God anywhere but in the earth, and sea and sky, and air, and virtue?
— Pharsalia 1.128

Millions of children trust God because they accept the beautiful magic of faith. Charles Ellwood, the sociologist, once wrote, "When a child is born, it is like a slate upon which anything can be written."

His analogy is good. Childlike simplicity has always been a precious notion. The painter captures it on his easel with a host of hovering angels or tiny white lambs. If all the world were so serene, what a wonderful place it would be.

But it is not to be. A child's simplicity evolves into teenage complexity, where angels and lambs no longer exist, but the metamorphosis does not always create exquisite moths. Indeed, the rules of behavior and the religious principles, once carefully inscribed on the youngster's mind during Sunday School and Catechism, often are either obliterated or consigned to remote cubicles of the human brain.

This may be an unusual comparison, but it applies: Learning to hold God's hand is *the reverse of potty training a child.* Parents may lead a youngster to the receptacle, lecture on why he should use it, and promise rewards, but training will never occur until the youngster accepts the system. When that happens, he consistently goes to the bathroom whenever nature calls.

Children follow an opposite ritual when learning religious behavior. Early on, most youngsters respond eagerly to Bible teaching. With joy and enthusiasm, they attend Sunday School. But, as they mature, an incredible number abandon the faith and often never use it again.

Maturing youth either permit their early training to lapse into meaningless habit, or else file it away with nursery rhymes, Aesop's Fables, and the myth of Santa Claus. Indeed, Santa's image in the expanding mind is likely to be more concrete than the face of God. This is easy to understand. Santa's face is real, but no one can adequately explain to a child where God is or what he looks like. And that's because our own adult perceptions are also hazy. What kind of answers are we able to give to normal adolescent questions?

> Who is God?
> What does he look like?
> Where is he?
> Why did he let Bobby Nelson die when he got hit by a baseball bat?

I recall the flabby responses I received when I raised similar questions:

> God is a spirit.
> God is our father
> We can't see God, because he lives in Heaven.
> God needed Bobby to be with him.

So the child becomes an adult who continues to worship a flimsy spirit up there and out there someplace; or else shrugs his shoulders, skips church, and goes fishing.

YES, VIRGINIA, THERE IS A GOD

*All right, how **does** one describe God?*

After half a century of attending church, I still find this to be a challenging inquiry. How can one possibly locate a spirit and describe it to people who demand evidence? For those who believe, no proof is necessary. For the skeptic, no proof is possible. The majority of people around the world *accept* the reality of a supreme being of one sort or another. Real atheists are rare; agnostics, not quite sure, are unwilling to take chances.

In spite of God's illusive nature, his *existence* is not an issue. Evidence of a superforce in the world is everywhere.

To look at the universe and declare it was developed by accident, or without design, is like saying my new car was created by throwing parts into a huge paper bag, shaking it, then driving out a sleek, efficient automobile.

Under no circumstances could the plan and the system of our world have happened by chance. As I sit on my patio this morning, surrounded by green grass, I witness a microcosm of God's system. The neighborhood is a sanctuary of finches, quail, and mockingbirds. A tiny hummingbird buzzes past my ear asking why I neglected to fill its feeder with red-tinted sugar water. A marauding roadrunner enters the tranquil scene poaching for baby birds that are too tiny to fight and too frightened to run. The protective mother quail conceals her babies in a hollow cactus then takes refuge herself until the invader departs with an empty beak.

Defying the December date, the trees still filter sunlight through shining leaves. By fortune of climate, they retain their greenery year-around instead of donning gorgeous Fall clothing like their counterparts in the frigid Northland.

MAN VERSUS SPIRIT

It may seem strange that the architect of this magnificent universe — of this synchronized system — has never been seen; that no one has ever observed his face. Even in the pre-Christian era when God presumably was sprinkling miracles on the Children of Israel, his face was obscured.

He was"...a cloud by day and a fire by night."
"Any man that sees my face shall surely die."

Those are very logical statements, because *God had no face then and he has no face now.* If you need to conjure a human image, that's fine, but remember, the symbol is not God. He has no physical body. He is not black, nor is he white. He is not man, nor is he woman. God is a spirit, and because spirits are beyond our experience he is beyond our comprehension as well. The late Bishop James A. Pike of the Episcopal Church grasped the truth when he said that God is not "out there or up there someplace. He is everywhere."

Yet, *what* is he? *Where* is he? Someone once described God's spirit as a great blue ocean. Each of us is like a tiny cup of water poured into that ocean. Gradually the cupful blends into the vastness of the sea. But it is always there. Its qualities and its individuality remain unchanged even though it is now but a minute portion of a greater whole. We are not God, but our minds are a small, unique part of a great universal whole. If we can accept that comparison, we are on the threshold of understanding God's relationship to us. Even if we cannot see him, he is always present, around us, and within us. A part of our mind.

Consider this: We may never take time to count the stars at night, or stand hypnotized in a forest of golden aspen, yet beauty forever surrounds us. In like manner, God is present whether or not we can see him, whether or not we acknowledge his presence.

To proclaim that God exists only as a spirit will offend the faith of many who want to rely on the conception of a physical body — a belief from a long-past childhood. Dissenters may quote scriptural text to refute my thesis. Still others will offer anecdotal testimony that they have seen and talked with God. I won't dispute their statements; I acknowledge that God does have ways of contacting people. His methods and his system are what we are striving to understand, right now. But our inability to see or to touch the living God need not slam the door on our faith or put a clamp on the power and strength of prayer. Even without scientific infallibility, we can confidently weave the fabric of God's spirit into our own. Indeed, it probably is there already, waiting for us to discover its secrets and to shine its healing rays on our thoughts and on our behavior.

To find God — to discover his power and use it in our lives — is not an impractical dream. It can be done.

> What a refreshing experience it would be to sit down, whenever we wish, wherever we are, and have an inspiring chat with the architect of our souls.

CHAPTER THREE

SHOW US A MIRACLE, LORD

Whatever a man prays for, he prays for a miracle. Every prayer reduces itself to this, "Great God, grant that twice two be not four."
— Ivan Turgenev

A friend once said to me, "I always carry a silver cross in my pocket, but I don't get *sticky* about religion." Like him, most of us have a token belief in God. Our perception of him may be fuzzy, and our relationship with him apathetic, but we carry around our little symbols. This indicates we either do believe or else we aren't willing to take a chance on being wrong. **Just in case there is a God, you know.**

If the masses are mere token believers, we all need a jolting shock.

What would happen, I wonder, if God would suddenly drop a giant-size miracle on us? That's how he supposedly got Pharaoh's attention when Moses was trying to herd the Children of Israel toward the promised land. If the Bible is accurate, God hit the Egyptians with famine, disease, grasshoppers, and a host of nasty maladies. For a few days after each strike, everybody on the Nile trembled with terror. But fear of those miracles — if indeed they were miracles — quickly dissolved like sugar in a basin of warm water.

How might *we* react to such displays of omnipotence? Would we shout, "By golly, there is a God!"; or, would we slowly shake our heads and mark off the event as a neat trick — like a magician's rabbits?

On a recent Sunday, my wife and I joined several other couples for breakfast after church. Our friend, Tom, was unusually quiet that morning as we sipped coffee and waited for our bacon and eggs. Suddenly his booming voice startled us.

"Will," he said. "I want to ask you something. It is true that we can move mountains if we have the faith of a mustard seed?" (Luke XI, 9-10)

Before I could even pretend I knew the answer, he asked, "Can I have whatever I ask for in prayer. Anything I ask for?" (Mark VII, 7-8)

Then he stared at me with expectation as though I were an Eastern Guru in possession of all knowledge. For a moment, my mind straddled the fence that divides ego from honesty while my mouth prepared to unleash a flock of cliches — ready-made answers from the years I spent as a preacher's kid in the parsonage.

But a voice inside cautioned, *This is over your head, fella'. You'd better pass.* My mouth obeyed.

At that time, this book was not yet a seed — not even a mustard seed. But in the years since then I have pondered Tom's questions, wrestled with my own thoughts, and examined stacks of research to learn whether prayer can indeed move mountains, and whether, indeed, we can...*have whatsoever we ask in prayer.*

Who knows, maybe this book was conceived, subconsciously, at that startling breakfast session.

HOPE BEYOND REASON

Unreasonable expectations can lead to unparalleled frustration. Because most of us were taught that God can do whatever he wishes — even move mountains — we are preconditioned to believe in his omnipotence; therefore, we often make preposterous demands on his generosity.

Pretend you are falling from the roof of your house. An inevitable prayer bursts spontaneously from your lips, "Please Lord, help me."

If you should drop into a nice soft haystack, you perhaps should thank *God for the coincidence,* but not for thoughtfully placing a haystack as a cushion beneath your fall. Either that haystack is usually under your roof, or one was temporarily placed there for some purpose other than saving your neck. **God had nothing to do with it.**

In April, 1989, Bangladesh was in the throes of a crop-killing drought. Hungry citizens across the land prayed for rain. Believe it or not, within a few hours, torrents and tornadoes devastated the country. Thirty five people were killed and a thousand injured. Could one argue that the prayers brought a miracle? And if so, should a miracle from the almighty create havoc for innocent people?

I once prayed for a special position in my company. I didn't get it. Years later, from a more objective vantage point, I arrived at this truth:

> *My prayers were futile. God could not have influenced the corporate vice president to stuff me into that job.*

Another example: You have just received a letter approving, or denying, your application for a bank loan. While you open it you silently pray, "Please God, let it be *yes.*"

Can prayer alter a letter that is resting in your mailbox? The loan committee has already determined your eligibility, and God can't change it any more than he could influence my promotion at Land 'O Lakes.

Consider this carefully: Would you really jump from a second story window and shout, "Catch me, God?" **Please don't try. It's a long way down, and there is an abrupt stop at the bottom.**

Is it practical to handle a poisonous snake and expect to be spared from its venomous bite? Of course not, although scores of deceased practitioners have tried it.

It is illogical to believe that God is forever in the driver's seat, that he can adjust the thoughts of a banker, cleanse the venom of a snake, or remove the impact of a fall. But one thing is assured: God will answer your prayer. It may not be what you expect, or even what you want, but he will return your call. (Jer. 33:3) Admit it, that's more than we sometimes get from our friends, or from the guy in the office down the hall.

IT'S JUST NOT FAIR

"Why me, God?" is an age-old question. Kind, loving and devout people so often get hurt, while the unworthy go unscathed. A child is gunned down in the school yard, and the pervert escapes. A chronic drunk staggers away from a car accident, but the parish priest is crushed to death in the other vehicle.

Contrary to myths and some reported miracles, God's laws are not selective. If snarled traffic caused you to miss a plane that later crashed, it was not divine intervention that saved your life. It was the coincidence of snarled traffic. A swirling avalanche does not distinguish between the honest and the crook. Like the *quality of mercy*, tragedy and joy descend on the just and the unjust alike. A world safe for the righteous might sound like Utopia, but it can never be. Tumors grow on any kind of flesh, under any color of skin, whether or not the victim believes in God and loves him.

My good friend, Al, had cancer. His doctor was optimistic. "An excellent chance for complete recovery," the physician said.

We prayed for Al, long and diligently, but his condition grew worse day by day. Then we began to pray for his early death. Knowing that the family insurance was not paying the bills, we asked for a fiscal miracle — an insurance loophole — a charitable intervention. Some may even have prayed that Al's wife, Doris, would win the Arizona lottery. A request like that sounds reasonable — a good way for God to show his mercy and his power. Al died when he was ready. He didn't want to die. He hung on tenaciously. Doris' money nearly ran out. There was no insurance loophole, and she didn't win the lottery. Not one of us could truthfully say his or her prayers had been answered.

A man drowned some time ago in the Southwestern part of the United States. Legally or not, the undertaker released the body to an evangelist and his wife who believed they could create a modern-day Lazarus. The couple prayed over the victim's corpse for several days, but eventually returned it to the mortuary, still a corpse.

Some unusual things do happen that seem to be supernatural, although I'm not sure they are real, honest-to-goodness miracles. The definition of a miracle is important. And our acceptance or rejection is no doubt colored by what we *want* to believe.

Perhaps we are more be be commended than condemned for giving God benefit of the doubt. When a coincidence occurs and our prayers seem to have been answered, we exclaim, "God granted my wish," but if the haystack doesn't appear under the roof, we lament, "It was not God's will for it to happen."

CHIN UP - THERE'S STILL HOPE
Take heart. Things are not as black as I have painted them. God is a fair and willing spirit who can influence our environment — a spirit with strengths and with limitations. He has built a remarkable system. By adhering to its principles — *let me say that again* — by adhering to its principles, our lives can be filled with unusual phenomena that do resemble miracles. We can actually learn what to expect from God, and by learning it, we can eliminate from our thoughts that awful cliche: *My faith just wasn't strong enough to make it happen.*

Friend Tom's second question that Sunday morning intrigued me: "Is it true that I can have whatever I ask for in prayer?" Stated accurately, the text is, "Ask whatsoever you will in my name and it shall be done onto you." This is a promise of personal power. Somehow, in spite of its *blue sky*, this verse has more practical potential than shoving heavy mountains around from one place to another.

Struggling with this New Testament text catapulted me into a long, rewarding quest for answers. During my odyssey, I confirmed what I had suspected from the beginning:

> *We rely on prayer, in a superficial way, but fail to use its full potential.*
> *We wish prayer could be more predictable, more consistent, more effective.*

We do indeed delegate our praying to the parish clergyman.

These problems can be overcome. By exploring God's system, and by acquiring insight into its miraculous machinery, the *Tom's* in our world will see that prayer is a tool, a natural component of God's program. Once we turn that tool into **prayer with power,** we shall no longer need to nag him with that worn-out challenge:

**Come on, God, do something for us.
Show us a miracle.
Make it easy for us to believe.**

CHAPTER FOUR

AND GOD SAID, "THAT'S GOOD"

And then the Great God Almighty
Who flung the stars to the most far corner of the night,
Who rounded the earth in the middle of his hand;
This great God...kneeled down in the dust toiling over a lump of clay
Till he shaped it in his own image;
Then into it he blew the breath of life, and man became a living soul.
— James Weldon Johnson

An enthusiastic young teacher was being interviewed for a science-teaching position in a *Bible-belt* community. The school superintendent asked, "Do you teach evolution or the Genesis story of creation?"

"You name it," the applicant said, "I can teach it either way."

Six days or a millennium? The *Big Bang Theory* or James Weldon Johnson's beautiful interpretation? How did our universe come into existence?

As the science teacher was probably implying, "Does it really matter?" The important truth is that *the earth is here and we are on it.* A wise person once said:

> *I don't need to know who dug the well or how deep the hole. I only know the water quenches my thirst — and that's all I ask.*

A GOOD WEEK'S WORK

If God built the earth in only six days he put in a strenuous week. If it took him millions of years, he deserved a good rest.

The mysteries of nature forever intrigue me — just as they have fascinated millions of others through the centuries. My contemplation does not flow through a scientific mind so much as through the eyes of a poet — or romantic, awestricken by the wonders of the world. To smell a flower or watch a bird in flight makes me tiptoe in God's majestic presence.

But this earth is more than a mysterious Paradise. It is dynamic testimony to a well-conceived plan — plants and animals locked into a scheme like finely-trimmed pieces of a jigsaw puzzle. Thick, rough bark insulates giant trees in the forest. Parchment-like skin enfolds tender onions in a blanket of rich, black soil. Heavy fur shields a bear from biting cold. Harsh scales waterproof fish against the sea that supports them. Gases in the air, mixed in exact proportions, support life in plants and animals alike.

Blood flows through our veins cleansing and nourishing life-sustaining organs. In bright light our pupils close to protect delicate membranes within the eyes. We feel warm, but perspiration stablizes our body temperature. Our minds absorb the scenes about us, and file details in the intricate folds of the brain.

The human ear is a unique mechanism that God never bothered to patent. The middle ear, an air space of hollowed-out bone behind the eardrum, contains three movable bones that transmit vibrations from the drum to the inner ear. Thousands of tiny hairs in the inner ear, tuned like piano strings, translate motion into electrical impulses that enter the brain as sounds of speech or chords of music.

God built an instant communication system that jerks one's hand from a hot stove. He created delicate living organs and folded them gently into compact body cavities.

He puts out the moon and stars at night and hides them by day. Through cloud-filled skies, magnetic fields, and bewildering lights, God's birds fly unerringly to their Capistranos. Monarch butterflies drink juice from the milk weed whose poison brings instant death to any creatures that devour them. The chameleon changes color at will and blends with its surroundings. The spotted fawn languishes safely amid splashes of sunlight in the forest.

The plants in my office turn their leaves toward the window. God's hand does not turn them. They are tuned to his system — in harmony with nature and its ubiquitous laws. It is a system so fascinating it beckons scientists into the nooks and crannies of the universe with a continuous question on their lips: "How did you do it, God?"

As a teenager I often reclined on a hillside in the Black Hills of South Dakota watching evening shadows chase sunlight up the rocky slope of a nearby mountain. At a precise moment when sun and shadow reached the peak together, the night turned dark and very still. Above the silence I could hear voices from an unseen choir:

Fairest Lord Jesus, Ruler of all Nature.

Our world comprises billions of complex inventions that are beyond comprehension. Don't try to count them. Even in an entire lifetime, it cannot be done.

And if it could be, we'd need a new word to describe the sum.

AND WHAT IS MAN...?

In the early days of creation, when God was a *King without subjects,* plants and animals either adapted to his laws or they perished. His methods for maintaining balance were often harsh: a forest fire, a flood, or a prolonged drought.

Without the power of thought, animals instinctively learned the simple acts of survival — stimuli that directed them to hide, fight, or flee. They learned to eat health-restoring herbs, and to massage their wounds with a soothing tongue. Montaign said, "Let Nature have her way. She understands her business better than we do."

But, for better or for worse, God came up with a complex invention that has *often interfered with the smooth operation of his program.* He created the world's first computer, a thinking brain, and planted it in human beings. Then he let them borrow his tools: chemistry, biology, physics, gravity, buoyancy, balance, light, heat, nutrition, inertia, electricity, radiation, pressure, and scores of other implements. Free of charge he lends Earth's materials to his people — assets by the millions: chemicals, minerals, fuel, water, and food.

By accident or experiment, people discovered the infinite secrets that God had tucked away in clever hiding places, and developed them for their own comfort: stable sources of food, comfortable housing, warm clothing, rapid transportation, and destructive survival weapons.

People took over the world, made themselves at home, and often dirtied their nest in the process.

WHICH OFFICER ON THE BRIDGE?

My childhood and adolescent training imprinted a maxim on my mind. It says, *God is forever in command.*

But somewhere in my life, *early training* collided with *subsequent experience,* and some challenging questions ejected from the crash:

> **Why are God's hands tied when there is obvious corrective action needed?**
>
> **Why doesn't he help us when we need him so badly?**
>
> **Why doesn't he clobber the people who are messing up his universe?**

Maybe it was to explain these things that someone concocted the theory that God is dead. After all, if we could dispose of him we could do as we please, and not feel guilty about polluting the air we breath and the water we drink. If the creator has passed away, we automatically acquire squatters' rights to the whole darn place. Right?

GOD IN THE SHADOWS

Fortunately, most people say, Wrong! Not too many believe that God has left us.

Not many want to believe it. That's because people are strange and inconsistent animals. Armed with great knowledge and uncounted inventions, they assert their independence — the right to do their thing — but they still demand the protection of a God who lives on high.

Dear God, please put a haystack beneath my roof.

God has given us a frightening array of liberties and we take advantage of him.

We are much like a teenager who wants to stay out all night and have the car whenever he pleases, but still comes home for meals, shelter, and cash when he needs them.

Take care of me, God, but don't ask anything in return.

THE REVELATION

Society is operating just as God planned it, but it probably is not performing at a level he had hoped for. When he cut the string that launched the universe, he relinquished control over his creatures. That's right. He let go. He expected people to explore and tinker with the design, modify it, but always to live within the rules he established. He made survival an intellectual endeavor with God playing the role of Observer. That's his style. He can no longer cradle our fall. What goes up must come down, sometimes with a vicious thud.

But God's laws were never meant to harm us. He wants us to understand them, to use them for growth, joy, and safety. Prayer is the access to revelation and adaption.

The most powerful prayers, therefore are:

Make me a strong individual, responsible for my actions.

Help me to accept the results if I ignore your scheme.

Most of all, give me power to make good choices and wise decisions.

God authorizes us to write the script for our lives. When we harmonize the text with divine laws, we shall no longer need to prop up our faith with false beliefs like:

**My faith wasn't strong enough; or,
God was testing me with sickness.**

THE RHYTHM OF THE UNIVERSE

It is apparent that God built some *chancy* factors into his plan, but we have to live with them. For example, a million male sperm — all different — are released in the female tract. Only one will determine the future child's characteristics. God does not select the winner. (The production staff at Chrysler might criticize God's lack of quality control, but century after century, he has produced some remarkable people — quite by chance.) This is his *natural system* at work.

God could manage his vast empire in no other way. All living things are tuned to the rhythm of the universe.

Another example: A shade tree in my back yard can't live much longer. Three dead brances droop from its dying trunk. God does not intend to cut them off. And I hope he doesn't expect me to do it. He is finished with that old tree. If lightening strikes its inert limbs, so be it. Early on, he made arrangements for its replacement. Every Spring other trees in our neighborhood spread thousands of seeds around the yard. One of those seeds eventually will replace my dying shade. This is the natural system at work.

God gave us humans the ability to think and evaluate, with concomitant responsibility for the things we do, the decisions we make, and the places we go. A family of happy tourists obliterated in a fiery crash caused by a runaway truck was not part of God's plan. Those tourists chose to make the trip and enjoyed preparing for it. The machinery involved in the tragedy was invented by man. It used the laws of mechanics and energy, the infallibility of gravity, and the heat of flames. This is the natural system at work.

Joseph Conrad once wrote a play titled, *Lord Jim.* After a shipwreck on the Island of Patusan, Lord Jim marries

Hello God, Am I Getting Through

Jewel, a native woman who cannot comprehend Jim's culture. One day, Jewel asked, "How many Gods do you have, Jim?" When he answered, "One." She protested, "Oh, one God is not enough. There are too many things to do." An old Protestant hymn carries a significant line: *His eye is on the sparrow and I know he watches me*. That's a comforting thought, but don't be caught smug in its web. God expects each of us to be alert for his own well-being, responsible for his own conduct, and content to accept the consequences for his behavior. For example: If I choose to program immorality, dishonesty, and hatred into my mental computer, be prepared to pay the consequences for misuse of the mind. If I choose to abuse alcohol, wave bye-bye to the liver. If *I've just gotta' have another cigarette*, say "Hi" to lung cancer. If I engage in a wild sex orgy, expect the possibility of a disease that might terminate my life.

I am not saying these things are either right or wrong. I am saying that individual choices abound in a well-charted universe. Cancer and sclerosis are not in God's plan. AIDS is not in his plan. Cause and effect are. God simply cannot be forever checking every link and kink in his universe. That would be an impossible management task.

LOVE IT; DON'T LEAVE IT

If there are flaws and imperfections in the divine plan, we nonetheless live in a magnificent place — not always predictable, not always understandable. When catastrophe strikes, as it frequently does, it is either cause and effect, or random action at work within the totality of God's extravagant composition.

Are we, then, but helpless pawns with cards stacked against us? Not at all. Later in the book I shall offer what may seem a contradictory thesis in favor of prayer — and even acknowledge that *special attention can be acquired from the universal mind*. But I shall not withdraw my statement that success and survival, properly defined, require an understanding of God's methods and a commitment to live within the framework of his laws. If we wish to ignore the rules, that's a personal decision. But, ignore the law of gravity, and boom! We have already discussed the outcome. Ignore the law of love, and — although less dramatic — the results are equally calamitous.

IS GOD'S WORK REALLY DONE?

I once heard a lady speculate that God has not finished his task, that six days — or six million years — was not enough time to complete creation.

"Even on his day of rest," she suggested, "God must have looked down and said, 'That's good. Probably not good enough. But good. And it will have to do. Time has run out on me.'"

So, the lady suggested, "He pulled the string and let it fly, hoping to correct the shortcomings as he went along"

That may be fantasy, but it is an interesting thought. True or not, be assured that God did not abandon his plan or his creatures. Somewhere his will is programmed into a giant computer that steers the course of the universe. *God's system,* I like to call it.

He planned it; he provided for its regulation; and he gave it to us — for better or for worse.

And then he added prayer so we could communicate with him. Learning how to *ring him up* is our power-link to safety, serenity, and harmony in an imperfect world.

CHAPTER FIVE

THE SUBSTANCE OF THINGS HOPED FOR

There lives more faith in honest doubt...than in half the creeds.

— Alfred Lord Tennyson

Newspaper polls may be less reliable that the size-label on a pair of cheap shoes, but they do provide the best measure available for popular beliefs and attitudes.

In 1989 United Press International conducted a national survey on religious beliefs. The poll revealed that 94 percent of the American people believe in God. Seventy-seven percent think they have a *good to excellent* chance of going to Heaven.

In spite of a plus-or-minus five percent error in the poll — and a lot of halfway believers being included — I infer that millions of people yearn now and then for the soothing power of religion.

Their yearning is not hopeless. Out there, somewhere, is an invisible force that people can call on for support. It lies beyond the neatness of the scientific method. It defies even the best minds to be completely logical.

Therefore, at this critical point in my writing, I suddenly go **bump,** and abandon reason because I must. There is no way to substantiate the mystery of God's spirit. It is beyond proof. It defies explanation.

Yet, 94 percent of the American people acknowledge its presence, and millions more through the centuries have also believed.

That's good, because, without belief, no one gets through to God; **with unrealistic beliefs, we waste our time trying.** Belief, however, must never be a stopping-off point, a way station. **We must go beyond to a thing called *faith*.** Belief is an acclamation. Faith is a process. Belief says, "I accept." **Faith says, "*I expect*...**I expect certain things from God, and I know he will deliver."

A STRENUOUS WRESTLING MATCH
Faith is difficult to define, hard to acquire, and tough to hang onto. Even Biblical characters, if the historical novel is accurate, struggled to understand it.
Faith is the substance of things hoped for, the evidence of things not seen.
At best, faith is acceptance of truth without evidence — a blind credulity. That admission alone is frightening. Who wants to anchor his life on a proposition without supports, or admits to having faith in a vacuum? Isn't this a clear example of intellectual dishonesty?
Not necessarily. The search for faith need not be a struggle, or dishonest either.
The problem is not lack of evidence. It is our inability to perceive evidence or to explain mystery. People who acknowledge the existence of God have already felt his presence without proof. This is belief. To go a step farther and admit an abiding faith is neither more nor less intellectually dishonest. Eventual discovery of faith and its power will provide all of the proof that anyone might ever need.
If we cannot take that step, if we cannot bypass the engrained and compelling insistence for proof, we shall never reap the full rewards of two-way communication with God.
Thomas Paine probably was not talking about religion when he drew his analogy about chasing things we don't believe in, but he certainly described human effort to reconcile faith with logic.

> **There is nothing worse than to chase something you don't believe in. Either you will quit running, or else you will go on chasing it because it is the accepted thing to do. But you will never catch it, because you don't believe in it.**

Paine's statement encompasses both the dropouts who cannot accept God because they can't prove him, and the half-way believers who find it expedient to stay in the race, but never plan to win because they don't expect to win.

Faith is the dial tone of prayer and the number we need for reaching God. Success lies in understanding it, accepting its limitations, and capturing its strength.

FAITH IS AN INSIDE JOB

God is available for the asking. His power is in the public domain. I've actually seen it capture and transform the lives of people, supplant hatred with love, replace conflict with harmony, and make each day a fulfillment of joy.

Many years ago I coordinated management development conferences at Lake Okoboji, Iowa. Although these were not religious gatherings, the sessions always opened with the group's singing, "How Great Thou Art." As the hymn filled the auditorium and floated across the lake, devotion lighted a thousand faces. Every person in the room at that moment overflowed with peace and serenity. For five or six minutes, there was no hatred. Only love. The strength of their united faith had the force of a powerful muscle. *If only we could entrench ourselves here,* I thought. *If only we could anchor this doubt-free moment when commitment has captured every human soul.*

FAITH IS A FRAGILE THING

Unfortunately, people tumble easily from the pinnacle when they return to the world of tests and temptations. Faith can crumble and leech away when we think we are being forgotten or when we have been betrayed. Life is filled with events that destroy faith: forgotten promises, thoughtless oversights, unintentional slights.

Once I took my young sons to an outdoor skating rink and promised to pick them up by five o'clock, well before dark. But I was unavoidably delayed. Night fell, and so did heavy snow. When I arrived at the rink, my headlights illuminated a lifeless winter scene, except for two small boys clinging to each other in the middle of the ice pond. I had let them down. Faith in their father had been shaken.

Another example: Our car consistently transported us across the desert and through city traffic for many years — trouble free — until one dazzling hot day when the engine failed miles from a service station. Till that day we never doubted our car's reliability. After that day, we did not trust it. It had let us down and our faith was destroyed.

Does God ever let us down? We think he does. So often we feel he has forgotten us on the ice, or in the desert; that he has overlooked our illness, or refused us comforts that should be ours.

What have I done to deserve this?
Why does he refuse me but reward my neighbor?

A PROCESS, NOT A STRUGGLE

It's time to free ourselves of faith-killing misconceptions:

That God is testing us with illness.

That catastrophe is God's will.

That God deprives us of our physical needs.

As a child I often heard pastors and lay leaders drilling fear into people. "Your prayer wasn't answered because your faith is weak."

How cruel to spawn guilt, an attitude that is the opposite of what God wants for us. He forever encourages us to ask for the right things, and to ask for them properly. Faith is a divine power drawing us constantly toward it. If we respond — seeking and yielding to its force — we can tap it, and it will help us. Acquiring faith a little at a time is much like a bird drinking water. It fills its beak, tilts its head, and lets the liquid trickle down its throat. Faith is not something that is *laid on us;* it is a process of *becoming, a movement toward a state of being.* As we temper it like slowly cooled metal, its brittleness begins to disappear. Small improvements bring great victories. Success breeds success. Strength builds strength. Faith bolsters faith.

Faith-seeking should never be a struggle creased with mental anguish. It should be a glide, not a squeezing tension. Ask any golfer what happens if he starts his swing by reciting the rules: **Head down. Arm straight. Eye on the ball.** When stress destroys the golfer's control, the ball often sails into the rough or dribbles to a ridiculous spot a few feet in front of the tee.

Faith is designed to relieve tension. It is the opposite of struggle. Unfortunately, we live in a boombox, fast-paced society that throttles the incubation of faith and stunts its growth.

Faith is nurtured in tranquil places, perhaps triggered by music, or inspirational writing, or meditation. Wherever it is, seek it out. Repeat the experience, again and again. Faith-building comes in quiet moments. Its strength is built by silence.

Someone else has expressed it so well: *It is only when we lie down in green pastures and walk beside the still waters that we can restore our souls.*

CHAPTER SIX

THE MAN CALLED JESUS

Often I am still listening when the song is over.
— Marquis de Saint-Lambert

When God planted his *tool of thought* in the human brain, he possibly expected the world — with the help of people — to fine-tune its own equilibrium, a sort of perpetual motion that keeps itself in a constant state of correction and balance. He probably never anticipated that *American superfunds* would be needed to clean up toxic wastes — that oil would blacken the pristine beaches of Alaska or Puerto Rico.

Sorry God, it just didn't work out the way you planned. From the beginning, people failed to understand your system. Their sins have ranged from devouring an apple to virtually destroying portions of the earth itself; from misdemeanors to unforgivable felonies committed against man and nature.

In his play, *Green Pastures,* Marc Connelly depicts God's displeasure with man's conduct on Earth. No longer able to tolerate evil and indifference, an angry God descends to Earth determined to scare the daylights out of people and make them toe the mark.

Mr. Connelly had an excellent idea for his play. But, even if God could walk on this earth, he would remove none of man's free-choice options. As I've said before, that's not how he does business. All lines in the drama of life are *ad libbed.* The Oscars are won by those who follow the supreme director's lead, for it was he who built the stage and it was he who designed the set where the action takes place.

THE OPERATING MANUAL

One Christmas morning my daughter-in-law was helping her three-year-old unwrap a Ghostbuster game that Santa had placed under the tree. As eager hands ripped open various components of the toy, Christopher's tiny voice warned, "Save the diwections Mommy."

A simple child inadvertently identified man's basic predicament on this earth:

He never received an operating manual.

Somewhere along the route, God must have realized the oversight and thought to himself, *Hey, these people need help. They have a performance problem.*

His corrective solution was both logical and theoretically effective:

Send down someone that people can relate to. Someone in their own image who can explain and demonstrate how the plan is supposed to work.

Mark Connelly notwithstanding, God sent his only son, Jesus — a baby, a man, and soon a martyr.

THE MASTER AND THE MYTH

At an early age, most of us were introduced to a *Storybook Jesus* on our mother's knee. We heard the Bethlehem odyssey read and re-read in Sunday School. As the story unfolds, Jesus advanced through adolescence to manhood. He became a remarkable teacher. He demonstrated unbelievable power. He surrounded himself with faithful people to whom he confided secrets and imparted strength. It is a lovely tale filled with joy, imbued with compassion.

But storybook tales are mostly fantasy — a game of **This might have been how it happened.**

Several decades ago, while I was teaching in a small college at Spearfish, South Dakota, my family and I participated in the mob scenes at the Black Hills Passion Play. One night when I appeared for a production, the director asked if I would fill in for a Roman Guard who had become ill. I was excited to do it.

As my horse plodded up Calvary, I experienced a moving sense of reality. It grew more intense as we fastened Jesus to the cross and raised his bruised body to an upright position between two thieves. Suddenly, lightning sliced the inky sky. With an explosive clap of thunder, the night turned black. Then a noiseless spotlight slowly illuminated the pathetic figure of Jesus on the central cross. It was so real, so impressive, that I wanted to kneel, instead of mounting my horse and dashing down the hill with the other actors.

Hollywood has also produced some quasi-historical and moving dramas portraying the life of Christ. And Raphael's painting, *Transfiguration*, is a masterful capture of Christ's ascension into Heaven. These productions are so visually persuasive that people often regard them as proof of the events they depict. The symbol tends to become the reality. Bland acceptance of a writer or artist's creative conceptions, however, is an idolatry that freezes the growth of faith. A personal relationship with God is the only way to tap optimum spiritual power. Jesus showed us how to establish that relationship. Failure to achieve it is like spending a lifetime in school without advancing beyond the third grade.

THE MAN AND THE MISSION

There is much confusion over Christ's mission on Earth, and his subsequent attempts to heal the human race. Traditionally, it is believed he came to wash away our sins — to die for us on the cross. I have difficulty accepting this thesis. It is too flimsy and irrational. It's a hypothesis translated into persuasive slogans. Indeed, I often wonder where the concept of **original sin** originated. Was it from the legendary fruit plucked from the Tree of Knowledge? Or was it when we first recognized nakedness? Or perhaps it was from sexual union between man and woman?

Even if the First Lady of Eden did influence Adam to open wide for a mouthful of forbidden fruit, it is difficult to make the inferential jump from Eden, to Calvary, to the Twentieth Century.

If original sin is a sexual matter — contamination by intercourse — I reject it even more vehemently. Procreation is part of God's system. It would be completely illogical, and totally unfair of him to create sex as a method — to set up a scam with forbidden fruit — then label it as sin for which Christ must give up his life on the cross.

If we insist that Christ's death absolves us of all sin — that it provided eternal forgiveness — then two conditions must be consequent:

The world has improved so little over the centuries that Jesus probably died in vain.

If Jesus' death gave us universal forgiveness, we indeed must have license to enjoy all manner of sinful pleasures then turn to Christ for perpetual intercession.

I cannot believe that Christ died 2000 years ago for sins I committed only last week. Nor can I accept the cruel hypothesis that an unborn child carries the stigma of original sin before it has taken its first post-womb breath. And my credulity level sinks even lower when I evaluate some of our arbitrary definitions of sin. Yet, I do believe in forgiveness. It is a basic element of the Christian faith. Forgiveness for our contemporary sins is forever valid, forever personal, forever rewarding.

I once had a friend who wanted to be a minister, but his early life had been pock-marked with lawlessness and shady living. "I can't be a preacher," he confided to me. "Too much muddy water has flowed under the bridge."

How sad. The barrier he erected between himself and a potential career could have been demolished like the Berlin Wall if my friend had turned to the therapy of faith and prayer.

JESUS STILL SHOWS THE WAY

Because forgiveness is so readily available, it seems a strange phenomenon that people withhold full commitment to Christ when the return on investment can be so great. Jesus is like a person who once walked through a city vainly trying to give away twenty dollar bills. People refused them because they thought there must be a catch to it.

God's road might not be easy, but it is possible. The Christian system merely tells people to forget their murky past and turn toward a brighter future. Jesus opens the door to all who desire admission. Christ demonstrated the practicability, the satisfaction, and the safety of God's system. His message, stripped of theological ambiguity, is simple and sound:

> Forget yesterday; turn confidently toward today and tomorrow.
>
> Step off the deep end and let God direct our lives.

Sounds frightening, doesn't it? And totally impractical. That's why it is so much easier to rest on the plateau of religious immaturity where one gives lip service to the faith, but never gives himself. Every generation has sought, even yearned for, the serenity offered by religious faith; but, like Al Hafed in *Acres of Diamonds*, we overlook the riches that lie waiting to be discovered in our own back yards.

By sending Jesus to live on earth among his people. God made a superior decision. Wisely, he provided the visual image humans need for creating a mental relationship. But even more wisely, he blended the spirit of God with the spirit of man. Every act of Jesus was based on that communion. The entire Christian odyssey focused on that phenomenon.

A Spiritual relationship with God, therefore, is the message of our faith. When we are blended together, all else falls into place.

> And it inevitably begins when the power of prayer permeates our minds and guides our lives.

THE FATHER AND THE SON

Several years ago, Barbara Mandrell and her children were seriously hurt in a car accident. "My family and I thanked Jesus every night for saving our lives," the country singer told a magazine reporter.

Hello God, Am I Getting Through

When I read Barbara's comment, I wondered why she directs her prayers to Jesus.

Why not go direct to God?

This question is not a stranger in my mind. As a young boy, I reasoned, **Jesus ascended into Heaven so there must be two supreme beings up there someplace.**

After sifting and sorting this profound idea for awhile, I realized I could not manage it alone, so I dashed into my father's study for a professional interpretation. My timing could not have been worse; Dad was in conference with an important parishoner.

Instead of retreating gracefully, I unloaded my inquiry. The men exchanged startled glances as though I'd asked an embarrassing question about sex. Finally, Father's Scotch brogue shattered the noisy stillness. "I say, Miller, this lad has been doing some thinking."

To me, he said, "You run along, son. We'll talk about it later."

We never did, but I was pleased to have been doing *some thinking*. From then on, however, I sealed my lips in case other stupid ideas should escape from my mouth.

Barbara Mandrell's prayer to Jesus broke that seal and caused me to re-examine the role of Jesus Christ in celestial and human affairs.

GOD'S RECEPTIONIST?

Still a youngster — a curious one — I finally decided if two people are *up there* running the heavenly kingdom, I should accept it and not trip over theological disputes and doctrines. Later, I even pretended that Jesus is an efficient, spiritually-motivated assistant, receiving and relaying messages at the heavenly switchboard. After all, he did say, "No man cometh to the Father but by me."

Jesus does bridge the gap to God. He is the link between us and the spiritual power we need for successful faith. It is Jesus who responds to the old protestant plea:

Open mine eyes that I may see
Visions of truth thou hast for me.

INSIDE CHRIST'S SALES KIT

When we contemplate Jesus, we are not dealing with an ordinary person. For three years he was a traveling salesman whose products carry infinite, unlimited warranties. He expounded rules that seemed implausible, but they made his mission possible, and other people's lives worthwhile.

Let's strip that message to bare bones to see how we can retrieve our proxies and establish our own transmission line to God.

When this man, Jesus, was wandering about Galilee, or confiding truths to his disciples on the mountainside and by the sea, he was not just talking about ordinary things like heat and light and color — or about forces like gravity and pressure and torque. He was prodding people to accept moral rules so stringent I tremble at their challenge; yet, so elementary I marvel at their simplicity.

Let's examine them:

Number 1: The foremost principle in the Christian faith is love.

Because love is a grossly perverted word in modern language, we need to clarify it. People profess to love so many things that real love has lost its beautiful meaning. *Love that joke! Love that car! Love that house!*

Those things aren't love. They are convoluted concepts of love that sprout from lazy expression rather than inner feelings. Balzac said, "Love is to the moral nature what the sun is to the earth." Love is a rich respect that passes back and forth among people. It has an infallible reward. It is a hot-line to God. Love and hate are opposites. Both can occupy the mind at the same time, but they have a destructive effect on each other. They can co-exist, but they are in perpetual conflict. Hate in abundance crowds out love. Consistent and compelling love banishes hatred forever.

In the comic strip, *Family Circus,* a child asked his mother, "Do you think you'll ever run out of love?"

"No," the mother said. "The more I love, the more I have to love with."

An open line to God is virtually impossible without a firm and consistent commitment to the law of love. It nourishes faith and raises the level of inner strength.

Number 2: Forgiveness is a powerful tool of faith.

Like hate and love, forgiveness and revenge are cohabitants. Fill yourself with one — either one — and the other retreats. Nothing is more healing in human life than the ability to say, "I forgive you" to the person who has offended you or done you harm; or, to yourself for being selfish and spiteful.

Forgiveness dissolves unkindness, jealousy, and hatred. It opens the communication line to God.

I once worked with a woman whose life was a full reservoir of love and forgiveness. One day, while a colleague and I were having lunch, this lady passed through a corridor at the back of the cafeteria. "Will," my friend said, "what does that woman have the rest of us don't have?"

"What do you mean?" I asked. I knew what he was referring to. I only wanted him to describe it.

"I mean her contentment. Then angelic look on her face. I've never known anyone so peaceful and happy."

Her name is not important, but what she possesses all of us can have by using the healing power of love and forgiveness.

Number 3: Jesus laid down the rule of turning the other cheek — asking for a second slap.

Temper and retaliation are psychological indulgences that interfere with the quest for God's system. The more one engages in conflict, the more often events occur that excite anger and motivate retaliation. Turning the other cheek a few times reduces the frequency of confrontations and equips people to handle disagreements with remarkable tranquility.

As I look back over the years, I remember many conflicts, but I can't recall what prompted any single dispute, or who won. Physical force and caustic responses provide temporary feelings of self-satisfaction, but habitual revenge is a cancerous habit.

It is a paradox of our faith that power resides in apparent weakness. To back off from dispute — to present the other side of the face — is a badge of courage.

One of the great revelations in my life was the realization that **love, forgiveness, and turning the other cheek,** are a trinity — all members of the same family. These three are the most important elements of the Christian code. They provide the serenity we crave. As we alter our attitudes toward other people, their actions and attitudes either quickly change or else lose their sting and their impact.

Number 4: More a promise than an obligation, ask for what you want when you want it.

In one way or another, needs are taken care of when requests are properly made. Of course this concept runs against the grain of common sense. How can anyone in right mind say, "Come on God, give me the things I need."

But that isn't what Christ had in mind. He never intended us to stop working, to be poor, or to become leeches on society. He only meant that worry and concern over material things is a waste of time — a drain on creative energy — energy that should be used for productive activities.

I've never been wealthy; I've had endless opportunities to worry about paying bills; but my worries never provided money. On the other hand, prayer has consistently produced the necessities of life when I needed them. Strange things — inexplicable things — have occurred. When huge expenses have faced us — costs we couldn't possibly meet — money appeared from unexpected sources on the day of reckoning. **When one quits worrying about monetary matters, monetary matters somehow took care of themselves.**

A young mother in one of my classes quit a lucrative job because she was "tired of being a slave to her corporation" and felt she could escape its fetters by acquiring a college degree.

"I made a silly financial decision," she told me. "Who in her right mind would quit a good job when she has a youngster to support?

Linda has prayed her way into the second year of college. "It's amazing," she said, "where help comes from. I think God will take me all the way."

> Consider the lilies of the field. They toil not. Neither do they spin; yet, I say onto you that Solomon in all his glory was not arrayed like one of these.

Ask whatsoever you will? You bet. I guarantee the principle works, but I don't know how or why. Certainly we have to labor, and certainly we should plan for economic needs, but that doesn't mean we should be obsessed with them.

> **Worry pays nothing. God's plan pays all.**

DON'T MAKE IT SO DIFFICULT

Jesus' principles seem harsh — even intimidating. And our perception of failure might add a load of guilt to the human soul. Maybe that's why people follow the path of least resistance, professing without demonstrating commitment. After all, if we go through the motions of Christianity, and perform its rituals, who will ever measure the success of our efforts or pull up the dipstick of our faith?

Too many of us avoid the Christian way as though it were a chain around our ankles. Maybe we've been overbombarded with verses like:

> **Straight is the gate.**

> **The gateway to heaven is more narrow than the eye of the needle.**

I wish, instead of making Christian living sound like a torture chamber, religious leaders would accent the simplicity of it all — the *let go, let God* concept and the rewards that accrue from that practice. Jesus is our guide, a mentor, showing us how to live. When we use him as our role model, marvelous changes come into our lives.

A leading movie actress was cited for a serious driving violation. "Do you know who I am?" she is purported to have asked the arresting officer. She apparently was unaware that **best performance** is not who you are, but rather what you do and what you stand for. **Best performance** is based on Jesus' blueprint for behavior. His system creates a magic blending with God.

That's why, when confronted by a difficult decision, I often ponder an important question:

What would Jesus do?

CHAPTER SEVEN

LEARNING TO LIVE WITH PRAYER

More things are wrought by prayer than the world dreams of.
— Alfred Lord Tennyson

Troubles hover like black clouds over the heads of unfortunate people. My friend, Mary, beset by financial and marital difficulties, one day exclaimed, "I'm damn mad at God!"

I understand how despair and anger were destroying Mary's life. She had prayed very hard with unsatisfactory results. Eventually, assuming she didn't deserve God's attention, she stopped praying,"...until he is ready to accept me," she declared.

WHO DESERVES TO PRAY?

That's an interesting question. Is it possible we should not pray until we have passed inspection? Can we be so unfit that we do not merit spiritual consideration? Should we stop praying until God is ready to accept us?

If you are one who harbors that belief, squelch it at once. It only delays the growth of faith, and may even terminate it. God does not seek us out; it is our job to search for him. After all, we are the ones who reap the reward. Obviously the return cannot be ours if we allow a feeling of unworthiness to bar the door.

Perfection — if it ever exists — is not a prerequisite for communicating with the holy spirit. Would a basketball coach expect his players to display athletic skill before letting them handle the ball or permitting them to enter the court?

I am not advocating denial of our imperfections, but blame may not always rest on our personal shoulders. We might have suffered social abuses that bruised our bodies and scarred our minds. Hatred, hostility, and lack of two-way love often take their toll on the human spirit. Everyone has blemishes from bumping into an unkind society.

A depressed person — one badly beaten down — cannot be a joyful Christian, cannot respond to the love around him, because he swims in a slough of bitter feelings, and carries a burden of hopelessness on his back.

Unfortunately there are not enough psychiatrists in the world to relieve the pains of those who hurt. And even if there were, the cost is far beyond the pocketbooks of millions.

But prayer is affordable, therefore it is the *designated hitter* for restoring mental health. Delaying its use only prolongs the agony of sadness and despair. Happiness is an end; prayer is the means to that end. It removes the scabs and cleanses the wounds of abuse, replacing them with hope, and joy, and serenity.

Prayer is the pathway to effective self-help.

TELL ME THEN, WHY DO I FAIL?

If prayer is the designated hitter, why is its batting average so low? Why do so many prayers seem to go unanswered?

In the first place, the fault — if blame is to be assessed — is not God's; it is ours.

The first step in rectifying the matter, therefore, is to make reasonable requests. As I have written earlier and often, some of the things we ask for are ludicrous even if requested in seriousness.

Example: A few months ago, while at a critical point in my writing, the electric power was interrupted, blackening the screen on my computer. Guess what I did, I prayed to have the electricity restored. It was an "Oh Lord, let there be light." A supplication with great fervor and strong personal desire.

Two hours later the lamp above the computer table announced that power had returned. But it was no miracle — not even an answered prayer. It was accomplished by four men who stretched a temporary cable on the grass behind our house. They were technicians trained to harness an energy created by God, but probably oblivious to the fact that God had anything to do with it at all.

Many prayers are doomed from the beginning because they presume to twist inviolable laws. Dumb prayers deserve to be ignored. Sometimes people even ask God's help in competition. "Lord, help us to win the game." How unfair to ask him to take sides. God could hardly dispense advantage in a contest between St. Johns and Gustavus Adolphus.

But, "God, help me to play my very best, to be a good sport, to concentrate on my skills, to play by the rules" is a valid request. Yes, God might be expected to answer that kind of prayer.

RUN-OF-THE-MILL PRAYERS

As a general rule personal prayers with flaws in them fall into three categories:

> Ceremonial prayer, like the formal rituals in church or at public events.
>
> Habitual prayer, such as stereotyped mouthings at bed-time or at the meal table.
>
> Crisis prayer — a frantic cry for help in time of calamity or great need.

When the Japanese Emperor Hirohito died, people throughout the world prayed for him. I don't know what they were praying for, and I often wondered if anyone ever monitored the results. I finally concluded that prayers were offered in respect for the deceased leader, but not for communication with the universal mind. It was a classic example of *ceremonial prayer.*

Often in church, or at home, we mutter inane prayers that have no meaning, no vigor, and no expectation. Mumbling in an unconscious state is as futile as asking God for impossible favors. *Habitual prayers* are a dud firecracker; a little fizzle, but no exciting explosion.

And all of us, of course, turn to God in time of turmoil. A pastor is never more needed than when crisis strikes. *Church attendance zooms when nations go to war.* The error is not in turning to God for help in these calamities. It's our lack of praying know-how. We are not prepared to make maximum use of his services. *Crisis prayer* is like cramming for an examination, or missing practices and expecting to play in the championship game.

THE EFFECT WEARS OFF

One of America's top motivating speakers — an enthusiastic, animated person — began to doubt his long-term effect on people's lives. Every year he addressed thousands of people, but finally concluded that his motivating ideas were landing on Teflon brains and failing to stick. Persuasive speakers have lighted the fire of enthusiasm in most of us at one time or another, only to have the flame go out as soon as competing forces move in to smother it. I once had a boss who is living proof of this contention. On Monday mornings, after a stimulating weekend seminar, he virtually bubbled with new-found ideas for things like listening, people awareness, delegation, or for whatever the subject of the meeting had been. He was a loving man, who sincerely intended to practice what he had learned, but Tuesday's pressure dulled his dedication. Wednesday's pressure further diluted it. Thursday's pressure wiped it out completely.

Consider this: Motivating speakers and religious leaders are all trying to cope with a similar set of human barriers: Daily pressures, taunts from others, negative emotions, and procrastination. Yet, some people do manage to change in spite of the obstacles in their way. I am curious about how they turn their lives around and buck the tide of professional pressure, surmount emotional barriers, and even slay the dragon of procrastination.

How *do* people defend their commitments and beliefs against the din of social interference? That question deserves an answer.

FINDING THE SECRET

I was impressed with Sylvester Stallone's portrayal of the fighter's role in the movie, *Rocky*. To train, he ran continuously along country lanes, up steep staircases and down again. He devoured strength-giving foods. He boxed and shadow-boxed day after day to improve his skills.

Most conscientious athletes follow rigid body and mind-building disciplines. It is called *unswerving dedication*. During my college days, I roomed with an athlete who sometimes toted a basketball for a week at a time, carrying it to class, dribbling it across the campus, manipulating it in our room. Cliff was rehearsing for what he hoped would be a flawless game on Friday night. In idle moments, his body and his mind were practicing ways to handle that ball. Each passing day its subtle presence made him a better player.

My friend, George, thinks his golf game slips badly if he doesn't get on the course at least four times a week. He would never think of going a week or a month without playing. **Yet that is exactly what we do with our plans for self improvement, and our efforts to learn the techniques of prayer.**

Why should we think it is easier to pray than it is to play basketball or golf? Prayer, like all other things, is a tradeoff. We cannot receive the things we want without giving up something else — energy, time, pleasure. The depth of the need dictates the intensity of the sacrifice.

If we want to succeed in prayer, if we want to capture its power, we must live with it. Remember that's how Cliff became a fine basketball player. That's how George keeps his golf game in shape. With the same kind of practice, conditioning, and attitude we can train to win with prayer.

LEARN THE FUNDAMENTALS

"Our new coach met us every day for three weeks before we found out he could smile," a high school football player once told me. His coach wasn't being unfriendly but he detected that his "veteran" athletes had never learned the fundamentals of the game. So, he hammered away until basic techniques became second nature to his players, and they in turn, were prepared for the rough and tough games that lay ahead.

Prayer is a communication process with its own set of *fundamentals*. Winning with prayer depends on proper use of principles that connect us to the universal mind.

Here they are:

Number One: The human mind is a magnificent part of God's system; therefore, all successful prayer must be transmitted through intense mental concentration. A vivid, dynamic thought planted in the mind during prayer will invariably reach fruition if it is in harmony with the tune of the universe. That is God's system of psychology.

Number Two: Prayer must be a consistent, on-going practice. You cannot put God on hold until you need him. People who communicate successfully with the universal mind go often to the well. No one can build a strong prayer link on an erratic schedule any more than a lad can build strong muscles by pausing to do an occasional push-up as he dashes through the living room.

Number Three: Prayers must be specific. Abandon the rote childhood expressions. Most of them are immature cliches appropriate for the youngster, but now vestiges of a passive faith. Fluency is not a requisite for power praying, but creativity, enthusiasm, and excitement are. I doubt that word-choice and grammar, sentence balance, or enunciation skills make a deep impression on God. It's better to stumble through with sincere requests for things we want than to rely on someone else's golden tongue. Besides, that someone else might be reading his prayer from manuscript, and — forgive me — I've always believed a prayer can hardly be effective if the pastor cannot close his eyes.

Prayers are not supposed to be sermons, or silly commentaries that sound like a newscaster reading the day's events. I once heard a man pray for seventeen minutes at a banquet. While he prayed for everything under the sun, I prayed that he'd stop and sit down. (I was in charge of the program.) God ignored both of us that night, proof that we have a tolerant and fair-minded Lord.

When you pray, clearly state what you want, or what you want to have happen, and why you want it. Ask for it in simple words. *Then, let it happen.*

Number Four: Expect results. Create a mental picture of the prayer actually being answered. If you ask for strength to face a challenge, visualize yourself bravely meeting that challenge. If you pray that an illness might be cured, witness your strong, healthy body. Expecting action enhances the effectiveness of prayer because it projects the power of faith on your mind.

Number Five: Don't try to make a deal with God. Don't spar with him. It never works. Parents may cave in to the begging child. You may badger your neighbor to borrow his lawnmower, but you cannot batter down God's defenses. He never wavers. His will is set in the mortar of natural laws.

Number Six: Don't make excuses for God. He doesn't need rationalizations like, "I guess he is punishing me." God doesn't do business that way. He doesn't punish us for sins or withhold forgiveness to enforce repentance. Nor does he entice us into trouble to test our will. We either fall into trouble by accident or we pursue it full steam ahead because we want to.

Always try to find the real causes for hardships or failure. See if you have stepped outside the system. Not all tissue can regenerate itself, so don't expect God to rebuild lungs burned out by smoke. He'll patch them up as best he can and help you to make accommodations, but lungs destroyed are lungs destroyed forever. You can't stop thunder after the lightening flashes.

Number Seven: Approach God with consistent requests. My biggest problem may also be yours: Asking for one thing while planning to get something contradictory on my own. Example: You cannot pray for moral strength if you aren't willing to cancel your fantasies of evil. You cannot ask God to help you rob a bank. Visualize the kind of person you want to be, then ask God to help you reach your goal. That's where he does his best work.

Number Eight: Abraham Lincoln once said, "The greatest battles of this world are won on the knees." The Bible talks about prayer in the closet. Perhaps both of these things are more figures of speech than techniques of prayer. Kneeling, hiding, and shutting the eyes undoubtedly create a mood for meditation, but only concentration, faith, and practice can open the line to God. There is, however, one absolute and universal necessity for effective prayer: Observe a quiet prayer period — ten to twenty minutes every day. Some people prefer the silence of their room, others an isolated spot in a park or beside a stream. A solitary bench in a crowded shopping mall will do as well, once the lines to God are opened.

Number Nine: Create a mental image of God. It will help you to reach him. Remember, one reason he sent Jesus as a person was because we think with brain pictures. God is a spirit, but many people cannot conceive an abstract God. They never attain a blending relationship unless they see him in their mind's eye as a person. When my daughter moved to Florida our telephone conversations were stilted and impersonal. I could not place her familiar face in the unfamiliar environment of her new home. Then I visited her. Now as we talk I can see her tilting forward on the kitchen stool, an elbow resting on the counter, and the telephone propped against her ear. Her face smiles at me, and I smile back. If a personal image helps you chat with God, conjure up the face of God as you want to visualize him/her:...black...white...whatever you like. God will not change, but you will see him so you can talk together.

THE POWER TO HEAL

God's universal plan always moves toward the retention or the restoration of good health. A tree seals the injury of its broken limb. Fever kills bacteria. In contact, broken bones immediately begin to knit. God cares and God heals. Prayer accelerates that process.

Healing through natural processes is an age-old concept. God provides herbs and minerals in the plan for creation that work in harmony with the immune and regenerative system of the body. Primitive people, and even animals, could identify pain-killing, body-healing plants. Drugs prescribed today are often derivatives, sometimes super doses, of those same health-giving plants.

But is there such a thing as spiritual healing? The answer has to be *yes*.

Documented cases show that prayer has healed uncounted patients. It has destroyed cancer when doctors have failed. It has kept people alive until medical help arrives. It has allowed people to hang onto life until an important, and climactic event such as an anniversary, has occurred.

God's biochemical processes constantly repair damage and keep the body's system in tune and balance.

THE MIND, THE BODY, AND GOD

The mind is master of the body. Disease and health have their roots in the thinking process. Prayers for healing seem to work best when the patient is involved, either physically or by being told that the prayer line is activated. On the other hand, I cannot testify that prayers fail if the patient is unaware of the attempted intercession. I just proclaim the chance of success is greater if patients are involved.

I prayed hard for Jerry. We prayed together even though he had had a stroke and lay helpless in his hospital bed. We asked Jesus to help him to regain his speech. To walk again. To let him stay with us awhile longer. We worked together for the ultimate miracle. He'd squeeze my hand when I talked to him. Although presumably in a coma, once he sat up in bed and kissed me on the cheek. And one evening, as I was leaving, he raised his good arm and vigorously waved goodbye. I was encouraged, but I did not know it was to be our last time together. Later, I wondered if Jerry had realized it, if he knew something I didn't know. Our prayers didn't restore Jerry's mind, but I am convinced they gave him a moment of inner strength, a fleeting sense of confidence to face what lay ahead. Above all, I know Jerry realized we were praying together, and I'll always know —

perhaps both of us will always know — that God acknowledged our communication.

Prayer stimulates body and mind to restore themselves. That is how God built his system, and that is how the system works.

Norman Cousins, James Allen, William James, and many others discovered and testified to this relationship. Today's physicians and surgeons are becoming increasingly aware that meditation can be both a substitute for and a supplement to medication.

Because so many faith recoveries have been documented, doctors are asking why prayer is so effective in both the operating and the recovery rooms.

And, yes, prayer sometimes fails as well, but I don't know why. Perhaps it is an inward problem that needs correction before prayer can do its work. Sickness has often been identified as a by-product of discord in a person's life. Doctors are acutely aware that stress contributes to a broad spectrum of disease from high blood pressure and heart malfunctions to critical lowering of white blood cells.

Inner healing may be needed before physical illness will disappear. Mental maladies — deeply engrained hostility, guilt, or depression over financial problems — may cause illness and deter recovery. Inner disturbances are like a deep flesh wound. A scab covers it until the inner repair has occurred. When ready, the scab separates, revealing a growth of new skin. Unless psychological sores heal properly — and first — mechanisms that repair illness and injuries cannot function efficiently.

Sincere prayer directed toward inner purging lets physical healing become a happy reality. As James Allen has said, "Man's wishes and prayers are only gratified and answered when they harmonize with his thoughts and actions."

There is a cause and effect reason for this phenomenon: God's spirit, working through the human mind, energizes the system. Ask for proper attitude, for God's command to correct psychological damage. He will respond to a patient who prays:

> Lord, my body is damaged. Cleanse my thoughts. Restore me to good health. Eliminate hostility, greed, and memories that shackle my mind. Let me forgive and be forgiven. Help me to tolerate the pain. Put the elements in motion that will repair my body.

Even if severe damage has occurred, restoration begins at once when prayer takes over. And this is what discerning physicians have begun to observe and respect.

MEETING GOD'S STANDARDS

When prayer has failed in my life, or when I have been refused the things *I know I deserve,* I too, have been *mad at God.* In the discouragement of failure I reasoned:

> God is not effective. He is a failure; or, God doesn't care about me; or (worst of all), God does not exist.

Obviously, I have thought, *I am wasting my time trying to talk with him.* Further and deeper evaluation, however, always has cautioned me, *Wait a minute. Maybe you aren't going about this thing properly.* I now know that several things were usually wrong with my attitude:

> My prayers were unreasonable, controverting God's will instead of supporting it.
>
> My prayers were rote performances without believe, concentration, or anticipation.
>
> My prayers were flabby and non-specific.
>
> My prayers were offered with lingering doubt.
>
> My prayers were filled with static from internal and external distractions.

If these faults are likewise your faults overcome them and prayers will go through with clarity, confidence, and consistency. It's as simple as saying, **Hello God, this is me on line one. I'm ready to talk to you now.**

CHAPTER EIGHT

RECEIPTS FOR COMMUNICATION

Who rises from prayer a better man, his prayer is answered.
— George Meredith

Once I heard a pastor proclaim, "I know that my redeemer lives, because I talked with him this morning."

That's easy. Anyone can talk with God. If, however, that person declares that God has talked back, a listener might slowly shake his head and mutter, "Obviously, this man is a kook."

How does one know if he has gotten through to God? How does one obtain a receipt for prayer?

I've often heard people say that God verbally directs their lives, tells them what to do, makes decisions for them. But do they really hear God's voice, or is it only an aberration — a figment of the imagination?

When I was in college, I had an experience that still haunts me. Students from a class in abnormal psychology scheduled a field trip to the State Hospital for the Insane. A patient on one of the wards had been selected for study. When we arrived, that patient was sitting on the terrazzo floor with his back against the wall, manacled hands resting in his lap. His muffled words and glazed eyes were overt signs of an abnormal condition.

"Your doctor says that God talks to you," our instructor said. "Is that true?"

"Yeh, all the time," the patient replied with a broad grin. Then he emitted a hysterical giggle.

"What does he say to you? Can you remember what he tells you?" A misty expression clouded the patient's face. He seemed to be struggling for an answer.

"What is God saying to you now?"

Violent anger replaced the man's misty look. He tugged at his restrainers, then shouted in a shrill voice. "Shut your mouth so I can hear him."

I am ashamed to admit that unkind laughter exploded among the students. Later the story spread around campus faster than the newest joke. And it was told as that — a joke.

Only a limited few ever declare that God has talked to them. Are the rest of us afraid to acknowledge two-way communication for fear of ridicule — or because others might think we, too, should have our hands manacled?

How can one tell the difference between God's voice and an insane aberration that seems to talk into our brains?

The way most of us avoid that question is to duck it. To feign belief quietly is easier than to shout against the laughter of a derisive crowd.

I shall not proclaim that I have talked with God, but I will declare he has answered my prayers and steered my destiny. If that is talking with God, I have done it.

EVIDENCE OF THINGS NOT SEEN

Prayer precipitates happenings that defy explanation, strange occurrences that are within God's universal system, but outside the realm of human comprehension. I do not believe in major miracles. I've said that before. But unusual events do happen in people's lives that cannot stand the glare of scientific scrutiny.

I wish there were space to describe the host of experiences in my own life that were clear receipts from God.

A few years ago, my car heated on an isolated road in the desert when the temperature was 118 degrees. I immediately sensed our danger, particularly because my wife's health prevented her from walking, or for even sitting, in the stifling heat. I prayed, first that I'd not panic, then that the door of assistance might open. But I never dictated the terms or the kind of help I wanted. That was God's job. Before I had opened the car door, a truck appeared from nowhere — a good Samaritan with ten gallons of fresh water in the back of his vehicle. We cooled the engine, added water and went on our way. Thirty minutes later, this time in a high-traffic city area, the engine heated again. My feet had not yet touched the pavement when the car began to move. Looking back I saw a young couple pushing us toward a nearby service station. I'm a kook, I know. God assured me on the desert that help would be along. He didn't tell me it would happen twice, but I never, never doubted the receipt for my initial request.

Coincidence? Fine if you believe that, but I have had so many coincidental interventions that I must attribute them to prayer: critically needed articles or documents that I'd searched for in vain. After prayer, they appeared immediately. Problems I could not cope with. After prayer they were solved at once. Bills I could not pay. After prayer, unexpected money appeared on time. And one misty afternoon when I was hopelessly lost in my airplane, I suddenly knew what to do. It was like a voice instructing me to climb into the clouds, something I had never done before, and something for which I was not trained. Soon, the instrument needle moved to the heading I needed for *homing* on the airport.

What about the haystack?

It won't be there when you fall from the roof. But a relaxed body and resilient muscles, cushioned on soft turf or billowy snow might be God's response to your prayer. He's done it. I've seen it. And it's completely within the system. And when all else fails, regeneration and healing are God's standard backup procedures.

KEEP A SCORECARD ON GOD

Keeping a performance record on prayers may provide a receipt for communication. It also helps one to improve prayer techniques and to determine what is reasonable and what is ridiculous.

Suggestions:

If a prayer has been effective, what did you pray for? Has the same prayer been answered before?

If a prayer is answered intermittently, why is there only occasional response?

What differences exist between the success and the failure?

Which prayers are never answered? Can you explain why they are not?

A scorecard of successes and failures improves communication skills and increases the number of effective prayers, largely because it makes us aware of what we can ask for and what can be granted.

One irrefutable fact should be a constant encouragement to all of us: Millions of people offer prayers every day. If there were no evidence of success would these people continue wasting their time? Millions of people have relied on prayer through the centuries. Could they have been so cruelly duped for so many years? Even if one allows for a certain amount of blind following — and much mouthing of words — there is a substantial amount of succcessful praying going on in our world.

Periods of skepticism and disappointment are bound to occur, but check these as possible errors:

Error Number One: We may be merely impatient. Other things in life aren't instant either. We might wait ten or more weeks for delivery of a new car, but we want an instant cure for physical ailments.

Error Number Two: We may be too specific in our requests. It is best to tell God the problem and let him develop the solution. If we pray for an exact answer, disappointment is likely when the result is not what we asked for. But we might be totally surprised to discover that something equally good was sent our way.

Dennis Fitch is an airline pilot who was riding as a passenger on the DC-10 that crashed in Sioux City, Iowa, a few years ago. Sensing imminent danger, Fitch went forward to the cockpit to lend a hand. He operated the throttles on the incapacitated aircraft while other crew members wrestled with the controls. His prayer was answered. He did not ask for a smooth landing. He did not ask for a miracle. He did not tell God what to do. He merely prayed, "Dear Lord, help us to get this airplane down."

I can't promise a receipt for communication one hundred percent of the time, but wouldn't fifty percent — and rising — be a wonderful response? As with all skills, success creates confidence and motivation. One good receipt brings on another.

A MANIC RELATIONSHIP

Once I used to chuckle when religious advocates advised, "Let go; let God." It's an impelling slogan, but who wants to relinquish control of his life? At the time, I surely didn't. I wanted to hold the reins myself. But, I admit, even then a mysterious feeling sometimes welled up inside. Not a painful thing like heartburn, but a gratifying, satisfying relationship between me and God. Remember, I said I hadn't wanted it; yet, it continually reappeared whether I invited it or not.

Later I learned to initiate the occurrence, and engage it almost at will. Its joyous appearance always told me when I had done the right thing; a total emptiness let me know when I had failed. That feeling is a receipt for prayer. It comes when we knock down the *Checkpoint Charlies* of our faith and establish an open line to God wherever we might be.

Learn to pray, and wait for the response. Watch for results. Identify the feeling, the sign, that you have gotten through. God's receipts are not always crisp Xerox copies, but be assured they are legible.

God is pleased when we acknowledge that we need help with difficult problems. Assistance is forever at hand from the one who wrote the laws of an orderly universe. He is not an absentee landlord. He is standing by waiting to serve.

SO...LET GO. LET GOD.

CHAPTER NINE

AMBULANCES AND GUARDRAILS

Man is continually revolting against an effect without, while all the time he is nourishing and preserving the cause in his heart.
— James Allen

This book is essentially about you and me — and prayer. But you and I are members of a greater society whose reflection in the mirror of God's plan is worth examining.

God's natural laws — gravity, light, motion, friction, and scores of others — are generally accepted, but moral laws are more ambiguous. They frustrate and confuse. How many people can agree on what's right or wrong about using alcohol, about abortion, about ethical conduct, to list only a few examples?

Here is an interesting puzzle to ponder: **Is morality the same around the world?** If not, can one drift in and out of sin by boarding a 747 to Tibet, or Teheran, or Timbucktu?

The right to behave as one pleases is declared to be a personal liberty. And that premise is not contrary to God's system. He has always allowed human beings to wander in and out of Eden at will, but those who make excursions confront awesome decisions, sometimes with dire consequences. They might not unleash God's wrath, but they could fall *out of synch* with the machinery of nature.

Benefits and/or losses are the direct result of the choices made. Strolling from the Garden to indulge in today's *anything goes* society may present some very real dangers.

People exhibit a preference for existential liberties — the right to be loose and free. Therefore, only a casual affirmative nod from society constitutes sanction:

It's okay for me to do this. Everybody else does.

Subtle advocacy from the loose and liberal entertainment world, for example, has profound influence on a broad spectrum of society. Too many celebrity personalities are setting standards for belief and conduct. Unfortunately, they also have nearly unrestricted access to mass media monopolies — television, radio, and movies — three powerful instruments for directing thought and behavior for millions of people.

A lawyer in a Southwest community publishes cinema reviews as a hobby. He rated the movie, *Partyline*, with an asterisk — very poor as a movie, but very high on the *sleaze chart*. To describe the show, the attorney wrote,"...sex begins before the credits end...just another cheap exploitation flick." After his review was printed, video suppliers were unable to meet public demand for rental copies.

Attitudes and opinions vary widely on what will eventually happen or not happen to a society with such obvious moral flaws. The question is a real source of concern to those who profess belief in established principles of morality.

> Some people genuinely expect that God will rise up one day to smite the world as he did Sodom and Gomorrah.
>
> Some expect that government and political authority should resolve our problems.
>
> Others give lip service to God's power to change the world, but aren't actively concerned about it one way or another.
>
> Cynics are resigned to the mess we live in and don't expect it to improve.
>
> Hedonists enjoy the free-wheeling society and wonder why anyone should condemn it or want it to change.

HEY MAN, TIMES HAVE CHANGED

People in the last two categories adamantly declare that conditions today are different. Moldy rules from yesterday could not possibly be relevant today.

Times have changed all right; conditions **are different.** Society is forever in a state of flux, economically, politically, linguistically, and technologically. But does God's system change? The rules Christ taught are imbedded in that system. To be effective they must be timeless, stable, and reliable, "...the same yesterday, today and forever."

One could hardly play football if an official suddenly shouted, "Hey, you. Ten yard penalty. You started running with your left foot."

And the player asks, "Where did that rule come from?"

"I just made it up. Ten yards."

If God's rules were so variable they would be useless. To revise them every decade, or to make up brand new ones for today's activities, would destroy the continuity of the whole program.

THERAPY OR FAILURE?

Matching the rules of God against the *anything goes* philosophy of contemporary society leads one to an easy conclusion: *The world, Dear Friend, is a wee bit rotten.* Teenage pregnancies, suicides, sexually transmitted diseases, child-abuse, community murders, serial killers, rape, and gang violence (need I enlarge the list?) have risen precipitously, hand in hand with lewd photos that grow ever bolder, motion pictures that depict horror and violence, and lopsided talk shows that glamorize and distort the **ideal lifestyle.** Alcohol and drugs threaten the lives of millions while advertisers dominate sports television — even high school and college sponsorships — with appealing commercials starring upbeat young people guzzling beer at glamorous parties. It is alarming that youth can grow up with no concept of high values, and actually be denied exposure to them at the logical location: the public school.

WHO MAKES THE RULES?

Moral codes dictate and control man's behavior. But there is seldom agreement on what these codes should be. They seem to be controversial, volatile, and variable.

Because men and women make their own rules of conduct, moral standards rise or fall according to popular acceptance — and people's willingness to abide by them.

Many years ago I heard a man read a poem called *Ambulance in the Valley Below*. I've tried in vain to locate a copy. (Sorry author, whoever you are. If I could have found it I would have given you credit.) Here is a brief, non-poetic precis of the verses:

Automobiles careening down a steep mountain roadway suddenly approach a treacherous curve. Many drivers, unable to make the turn, roll off the cliff into the valley below. A few residents clamor for a guardrail, but they are ignored because most people would rather rely on...*the ambulance in the valley below.*

The analogy is obvious. Every day we read suggestions for solving social problems with screaming ambulances. We keep asking, "What's wrong with that?"

When deep down we know we should be asking, "What's right with it?" There may be some among us — we hope so — who have begun to realize that our **"education solutions"** are causing social disaster.

> *Learn when to say when.*
> *Let's make equipment available for safe sex.*
> *Don't drink and drive.*
> *Just say no to drugs.*

It's a cruel irony to maintain expensive ambulances in the valley while bodies are rolling off the mountainside, or drowning in the quicksands of moral muck.

The fulcrum between idealism and materialism — between secularism and moral conduct — shifts steadily in the wrong direction. Decisions traditionally made on the foundation of human values and human ethics and human respect are now made on fads, finance, and distorted suggestion.

SAY WHEN, GOD

Will God ever intervene? Will prayer give his team an edge on the playing field? I fear not. God neither supports his advocates nor strikes down his adversaries.

My mother used to recite a verse that probably expresses the longings of many people.

Truth forever on the scaffold;
Wrong forever on the throne,
But behind the dim unknown.
Standeth God within the shadows
Keeping watch upon his own.

It may be comforting to hope that prayer and supplication will someday cure our social ills, but prayers for moral victory are a fruitless waste of time. So, as the popular expression goes, "Don't hold your breath waiting for it to happen."

But the good news is...

When people realize that life is being sodomized — when they begin to do something about it — a guardrail will replace the ambulance. It is a false and foolish assumption that there are no standards outside of the ones we set for ourselves. I'm not sure old Moses really found tablets on the mountainside, but wherever his commandments came from, he presented some practical codes of conduct that are the best, the most reliable, the world has ever seen. They create a dependable platform for important decisions and acceptable behavior.

I am not a crusader with a mission to change the world. I am content to hope that a new wave of conduct will one day sweep over us. Someday, concerned people — sincerely concerned people — will affirm, "Enough is enough already." At that point, God's game will turn around because his team will make it turn. But it won't happen **until the players themselves say, "WHEN."**

God's rules are a stable foundation for life. Their rich meaning has withstood the abrasion of time, but their application must be forever consistent. They cannot apply in one way to me and in another way to you. They cannot mean one thing today and something else a hundred years from now. They are inflexible, invariable, and universal. And they definitely are not an aspirin to be taken when the going gets tough, or a passing fancy to be heeded only when one has time for it. God's message should be worn bravely — not boastfully — on the sleeves of all who believe and have faith in their beliefs. Good news hides in the shadow of our murky society. As more and more people discover the value of blending with God, the score will tilt in his favor. It may be a slow process, because it depends on the strength of committed people, working collectively. As Edmund Burke said more than two hundred years ago, "The only thing necessary for the triumph of evil is for good men to do nothing."

Four goals must be accomplished, by hosts of people, before the good news will arrive:

> **Review the laws of God as taught and demonstrated by Jesus.**
>
> **Commit yourself to those laws with determination.**
>
> **Experience the reality of blending with God.**
>
> **Learn the simple methods for getting through to him.**

Faith and commitment are parallel forces that foment change. The appropriate prayer is for courage to fold the tenets of Christ into every facet of our lives. If sufficient people on God's team accomplish that, his will and his control shall abundantly prevail.

Old hymns probably cannot elevate the moral tone of society, but very often one of them expresses a pervasive truth. Hear this one. Hum it to yourself if you know it:

> *Brightly beams our Father's mercy*
> *From his lighthouse ever more.*
> *But to us he gives the keeping*

Of the lights along the shore.

CHAPTER TEN

THE HERE AND NOW

Ah, but a man's reach should exceed his grasp, or what's a heaven for?

— Robert Browning

No book on prayer can be complete if it overlooks the subject of heaven. I'm not positive about heaven, and neither are you, but I am willing to believe it probably exists. As a child I imagined Paradise was in the Black Hills of South Dakota, and that the tiny town of New Underwood was one of its suburbs. Now, I look back on my childhood simplicity with a smile on my face, but no regrets in my heart.

Many Christians believe a happy state of harmony with God is not part of contemporary reality, that it is reserved for the future — the hereafter.

That's poppycock. Harmony is here on earth — a place where God's will can blend with the mind of every person who both seeks his grace and is willing to make the tradeoffs required for finding it.

There is strong evidence, however, that eternal life is real. People returning from a near-death experience describe its wonders. Jesus promised "...to prepare a place for you." But we won't really know about it until the time comes. Recognizing the creative and constructive skill God has demonstrated, he probably tucked Paradise away on a distant planet in an infinite corner of the universe. Perhaps he reserves space there for happy souls who discover his will on earth — or perhaps for people who deserve a second chance after messing up their lives first time around. But Heaven, right now, is not my major concern. As long as it's not the Black Hills I'm really quite indifferent about either its location or what it is used for.

RATIONALIZED FAILURE
I have a friend who actually said, "I don't care about this world. I live for the hereafter. I know I'll be happy there." What a *copout*. What's wrong with being happy here? And now? Life is too rich to be squandered. If we fail to find happiness here and it turns out there is no life after death, we'll have blown every bit of our three score years and ten. But, if we find happiness here in harmony with God and his system — and if there is a splendid hereafter — we shall have enjoyed the best of both worlds.

MEANWHILE, BACK ON EARTH
The here and the hereafter? It's here that really counts. Life's greatest reward, life's greatest satisfaction, lies in reaching a warm, lasting relationship with God. But how does one really know when that is accomplished? How does one know when he is blending with the universal mind?

I've only partially answered that question. Let's take another look at it:

When the lines are open to God, the mind fills with pleasant thoughts, and the body fills with comfortable warmth. It is like a rushing stream through which flows love, forgiveness, trust, serenity, and a feeling of resigned satisfaction. The power of the mind seems to expand beyond its traditional capacity. Understanding and contentment supplant the dissatisfactions that usually dominate a soul that is out of touch. Some people break into song, or spend time in meditative thanksgiving. It doesn't matter whether you sing or keep it inside, you will always know when you have bonded with God. And others will detect it too.

Eventually, the prayer-minded person arrives at a point where life can no longer tolerate its separated compartments: a compartment for politics, for business, for family, for social organizations, and occasionally, a spot for religion when there is space available.

As all facets of life meld into a God-directed unity, the old ways and the negative attitudes break off and fall away.

IN THE EYES OF THE LORD
We hear much these days about civil rights and equal opportunity. Society has developed a philosophy that one size fits all, that we are all alike, that we all came from the same mold. This is a myth. The world is crammed with disparities that are readily discernible: mental ability, physical strength, economic abundance, political power, social status. In none of these areas can there ever be parity among people. Only religious faith can embrace the rich, the poor; the weak, the mighty; the dull, the bright, people from all walks who want to power their lives with a prayer-driven engine.

"Through me, O Lord, let thy will be done."

God still controls his world by guiding those who seek him out, by strengthening those who don't give up or compromise, by helping people to design their destinies with deep and abiding faith.

The preacher in John Steinbach's *Grapes of Wrath* displayed great enlightenment when he speculated:

> **Maybe a man ain't got a soul of his own. Just one big soul that belongs to everybody.**

ON SLIDING BACKWARDS
Now and then we may lose ground. We may skid a bit, and disturbing questions will arise. For example:

How can I forgive when I just want to get even?

Am I not entitled to an eye for an eye? A tooth for a tooth?

But, live with God long enough, and one soon learns that turning the other cheek is a superior weapon. The old rules of anger and vengeance are poison pills — cancers of the mind and soul. To fall short is human, but to despair is fruitless. Progress may sometimes be slow. Back-sliding may be frequent. But suddenly, in fleeting moments, we discover subtle changes occurring in our behavior, unusual things happening to our minds. Then prayer takes over and does its work. Even with our multitude of shortcomings, it directs us into a pathway of happiness.

WE HAVE THE BALL

It is clear that the initiative for working with God is yours and mine. He does not come looking for us. He wants us to seek him out. Jesus taught, "Ask and it shall be given." It must follow, therefore, that nothing will be given if we don't ask, if we don't pray for it.

God wants us to come to him and learn. Real success in life hinges on our ability to weave him and his power into the great, evolving script of our lives. He gave us incredible freedom: **the power to challenge his will against our own.** Who has the last word? That question has not yet been answered. But when we are in harmony with the divine framework of life, the question loses its relevance. Through prayer we arrive at the *here-and-now reality* impressed on the world by a Jewish carpenter from Galilee who cried out:

Not my will, O Lord, but thine be done.

CHAPTER ELEVEN

PERSON-TO-PERSON CALL FOR GOD
An Epilogue

Hello, God. Can you hear me? Am I getting through? It's been a long journey since we started this book together — a journey marred by a terrible tragedy, a severe heart attack, and life extending surgery. Thank you for courage, for strength, and for guidance through these troubled years.

(I guess I haven't told my readers to thank you, always, for answered prayers. Very important).

Life, like the weather, cannot be altered by man. Only you can really change things, and only you can help us to accept the undesirable things of life without harm and without complaint.

That's what real *power-prayer* is all about. Its ultimate reward is the effect it has on our personal lives and on our personal living. Someone else said it far better than I can when he suggested that **being is more important than doing.** *Being like Christ is the forerunner of all good deeds.* Christ puts values in our lives.

Although the process is sometimes slow, prayer does diminish selfishness, dissolve fear, and dissipate worry. Prayer purges unkind and untidy thoughts, raw desire, and selfish cravings. It implants standards of goodness and peace.

When I reach out to touch your face, God, I feel a surge of goodness within myself. My personal blemishes seem to shrink like a treated tumor. Not that they don't plague me at times with their return, but what matters is that you quiet the turbulence of the human soul, free the mind for creative thought, and play the rhythm of placid life.

I know how often I have failed, but you and I also know how hard I have tried. I realize I am not eligible to wear a combat medal unless I have felt the heat of the moral battle.

While I think of it, I haven't meant to knock the organized church, God — or its pastors. I grew up in the church both to clean it and to kneel in it. I can sing a hundred hymns from memory — all four verses — and I have listened to three thousand sermons.

But to qualify for the combat medal I had to establish my unity with you. To be worthy, my faith had to expand beyond the church just as education must reach beyond the classroom. It is in personal encounters that mysterious forces come together, spirit with spirit. It is like the measles. You can define the disease, and you can describe it, but you can't give it unless you've got it.

Prevent me, God, from falling into the pit of self-righteousness. That is one hundred and eighty degrees from my goal. Let my faith, instead, be a natural state that radiates from inside, not a veneer or a paint that covers up the old rough surface. Make me a new person whose life is launched on a mission of happiness, dedicated to helping others, knowing all the while that when I *am* a Christian, I shall automatically *perform* like a Christian. **What I am will forever condition what I do.**

So, thanks, God, for prodding me and sparing me to finish this book. Without your vigorous shoves I could not have seen it through.

And one more thing, God: Please keep a sharp eye out for our son, Bruce. He was so unhappy and mixed up when he left us. I know you can help him. And when you see him, tell him I'll be along after awhile.

Thanks again, God. I'll talk to you later.

—Will Turner

Will Turner

Mail Order Page

To order copies of
Hello God, Am I Getting Through?

provide the following information...

Ship to:
(please print)

Name:_____
Address: _____
City:_____State:_____Zip:_____
Daytime telephone number: (   ) _____-_____

_____copies of *Hello God, Am I Getting Through?*
@ **$5.50** each $_____
Arizona residents add **5 1/2 %** sales tax $_____
Postage and handling @ **$1.50** per book $_____

Total enclosed $_____

Make checks payable to:

Expression Services

And mail to:

**Expression Services
P.O. Box 1616
Surprise, AZ 85374**